INVESTING 101:
A BEGINNER'S FINANCIAL GUIDE FOR A RICH LIFE

The Basics on How to Make Money and Build a Wealthy Retirement

Erick Walk

TABLE OF CONTENTS

INTRODUCTION

Thanks for downloading this book. It's my firm belief that it will provide you with all the answers to your **Investing** questions.

This book has been written to help every individual looking for ways to save and make a lifetime investment. In this introduction, we shall have a look and will discuss several important tips for savings and investments that can be considered when developing a saving plan.

This includes:

Save Regularly

No matter how old a person is, it is important to put money toward saving and investing regularly, as the benefit of accumulated funds is one of the most important factors of wealth accumulation. Even if only a small amount of money can be set aside at a time, regular contributions to saving plans will grow over time and will result in the accumulation of funds.

Diversify

While saving cash is great, especially if the cash contributions are intended for a short term saving plan, it is important for the saver to consider several different saving vehicles. Saving plans available vary, but to take advantage of the many benefits available, diversifying with several different strategies is most desirable and may result in a greater saving. Each financial portfolio should include safe, conservative options for the security of funds, and more aggressive options for growth opportunity. Not every investment type is right for everyone. It is important for the saver to consider his or her risk tolerance and long-term financial goals.

Take Advantage of Tax Benefits

There are many programs and benefits available that will reduce the amount of taxes that are paid on a saver's income. The best advice is to seek out the investments and savings plans that offer the greatest tax benefits. Over time, these plans can result in great saving and lead to great financial growth.

Plan for the Long Term

Whether a person begins saving in the teenage years or as an adult nearing retirement age, the priority should be placed on a long-term perspective. It is important that short-term funds are available in case of emergency, but by committing to a disciplined approach to regular saving that is diversified and takes advantage of tax benefits, the funds will automatically be there in case of a financial emergency.

It can be challenging for families to find extra money to contribute to a saving or investment account. Living a lifestyle within, or even below, one's means may be required to achieve financial independence. It is crucial, however, that a specific plan is in place for an individual's financial security. Research into the many different options available should be conducted, and it would be prudent to consult a financial professional for guidance.

By using the above tips, the average person can be confident that their money will grow over time and provide for his or her family needs. The most important tip, however, is to be disciplined and consistent. Only then can the greatest rewards be reaped. Read On!

CHAPTER 1: WHY AMERICA'S YOUNG ADULT SHOULD START SAVING NOW

There is this sad reality about money that concerns the country's young adults - the millennials. It seems setting some money aside for future needs is the last thing in their minds. They are so comfortable living in the present that it never occurred to them to think about, much less save for tomorrow.

To them, saving money for future purchases doesn't make sense at all. Why should it be when they can easily pull out their credit cards and buy the things they want right then and there when they want to? Besides, the credit card's low minimum monthly payment that usually comes also with extended payment periods fit their meager take home pay perfectly.

They can't make sense of the idea of saving for a contingency that may not happen at all or may occur several decades from now. They believe saving money is something they will seriously consider at a later date sometime in the future.

What they fail to realize however, is that at some point in time, they will have to contend with tremendous financial obstacles they may not even be able to hurdle so easily. For one, it would be difficult for them to immediately land good-paying jobs after college, and we know too well that the meager pay from entry level jobs would only allow them to live a payday to payday kind of life.

Then, there is the burden of settling the huge student loan debt they have accumulated throughout their college days, which may take them decades to settle.

Many of them start living on credit, relying heavily on the use of their credit cards even for their most basic needs. In the process, they get caught in a never ending cycle of accumulating credit card debt and paying off these debts over and over again throughout most of their entire adult life. Decades hence, they are still unable to save enough to live comfortably in retirement – a dream every salaried worker works hard for to make it happen.

Unfortunately, most millennials hardly care about retirement. It is too far away for them to even start thinking of saving for it now.

If you look at it closely, millennials are simply replicating the bad habits of their 'baby boomer' parents who we know were struggling to retire because they neglected to look at the future and failed to invest enough to secure their golden years.

Because of their devil-may-care attitude, millennials are likely to face less-than-bright futures. According to a recent survey conducted by Google for 'Go Banking Rates', 42.2% of millennials age 18 to 34 have not saved a single penny for their retirement while a mere 29.8% have less than ten thousand dollars in savings.

The same survey revealed that only about 26% of these young adults below 30 years old have actually invested money on equities. In other words, majority of our millennials are missing out on big opportunities to become financially fit and build their retirement funds.

If you are one of these unfortunate millennials, this book is for you. It is high time that you start rethinking the direction you are taking. There is still time to avoid getting caught in the whirlpool of credit card debt where you may not be able to get out of easily. There is still time to start saving money to build a nest egg and set up an emergency fund for other unexpected contingencies.

Don't ever think that because you are young and retirement is still decades away, you should not save for it. There is no such thing as being too early to start setting up a retirement fund.

Ponder on this. If you start saving late, say at the age of 35 rather than 10 years earlier at the age of 25, you'll be missing out on 10 years of interest earnings on your money. If you decide to start saving and investing only after you reach forty years of age, you'll need to save 3 to 4 times more to be able to put together the same amount of retirement fund at age 65.

Think of it another way. If at the age of 25 years old you start saving a hundred dollars a month and invest it with a conservative 6% annual return, you will have over $185K by the time you reach 65 years old.

Saving money doesn't mean you have to strictly tighten your belts and forego all of the creature comforts you've been used to all these years. Saving is about spending your money intelligently. It is about keeping a constant tab on your finances to avoid accumulating 'excess fat' in your spending budgets.

The main obstacles why most millennials are unable to start saving and investing is because of the meager income that comes from their entry-level jobs and the burden of paying off huge student loan debts. There is practically nothing left from their paychecks to save. This should not hinder them though from starting the habits of saving and investing wisely and building their nest eggs early in life -- even in the smallest way possible.

Saving is about having the discipline to manage your money smartly. There are many ways you can jump start your own savings program methodically without putting too much stress on your current lifestyle. Start by changing the habit of saving only whatever is left of your pay check after you've paid off the rent and other necessities.

Instead, commit a fixed portion of your monthly paycheck to savings and have it automatically transferred to a separate savings account or a retirement fund. This way, you'll have something in your savings account before your paycheck totally disappears from your hand.

Here are more tips you can make use of to start saving immediately for your future whatever financial status you are currently in:

1. The idea of paying yourself first when your monthly paycheck arrives before you start paying off any of your bills or before you go on a shopping spree is the best way to force yourself to save money every month. Ideally, you should be earmarking ten to twenty percent of your monthly income for savings. However, if your monthly bills and other recurring expenses would make this impossible, then it is alright to start with something smaller than 10% as long as you make it a point to increase the amount saved each month if and when your income improves - until you are finally able to set aside up to 20 percent of your monthly income savings.

You should also make sure the amount you set is automatically transferred to a separate savings account or deposited straight to a retirement fund. The goal is to make sure you have some funds stashed away for rainy day requirements before your whole paycheck totally disappears from your grasp.

2. Cut the habit of buying on impulse, especially with high ticket items. Think twice before making any major purchase. If possible, sleep on it overnight before deciding to make the purchase.

3. Stop using your credit card or try to use it only for emergency purchases. If you can't, then at least use it sparingly. Don't forget that when you have running balances on your credit card, there'll be interest that will be added on. Besides, you are actually spending money you haven't earned yet.

4. No matter how cash-strapped you are or how tight your budget is, try to establish an emergency fund separate from your main savings. You can start with as low as $25 per month or any amount that will not be a strain on your budget. Your goal is to build up a cash reserve that is equivalent to at least 3 months your living expenses.

   This shall serve as your safety net that will help you cope with emergencies. You may end up selling some of your investments for cash prematurely if you fail to establish an emergency fund with sufficient cash for unexpected expenses.

5. Discard any money-draining habits you may have. Replace them with the habit of always looking for a cheaper option or bargaining for a better price before letting go of the penny.

6. Instead of hailing a cab or booking an Uber ride, take a public transport to get to your destination. You will

easily save around a thousand a month doing so. You may also consider riding a bike to work if you happen to live in a place with flat roads and no hilly portions.

7. Be mindful of your debts and your spending habits. Keep them in mind when you create a budget. This will prevent things from growing out of control. Start by listing down all your cyclical expenses and then figure out where you can cut corners and trim down the 'excess fat' in your budget. Scrubbing your budget to eliminate unnecessary expenses, while at the same time trimming the regular expenses to their minimum should be the cornerstone of every saving scheme to be successful.

   By being creative on your cost cutting chore like cutting off the discretionary expenses, you'd be able to reduce your expenses by as much 20% or even more. You can channel the money you save straight into your rainy day fund or better still, use it to pay off debts.

8. Augment your earnings by getting a second job or by engaging in a seasonal part time job. The more money you earn, the more you will be able to stash away for your rainy day requirements.

9. Map a plan on how to rid yourself of your student loans. Carefully study how you can come up with a plan to pay off your student loan debt. Explore all possible payment schemes with an eye for the one with the least amount of accrued interest. Find out if consolidating your debt will benefit you more. If there are student loan forgiveness programs available, make use of it to get out of debt.

10. Accumulate as much knowledge as you can about investments and once you are equipped with

sufficient knowledge, start investing your savings on select financial instruments. Inflation has a funny way of eating up your savings if you simply put it in an ordinary savings account which earns a mere 1% annual interest. With inflation at 3% to 4%, it's a matter of time before you lose a sizable chunk of your savings to it.

CHAPTER 2: MORE IDEAS ON SAVINGS AND INVESTMENTS

At the end of one's working life, it is good to look forward to taking time off and to be able to live comfortably on a lifetime's savings. It helps if your investments bring in good returns. Everyone everywhere is dealing with the effect of inflation and a fluctuating market. The question is, does your money bring in good benefits, or is it time to change to a different, more beneficial scheme? Getting financial advice is the best option. Should a helpful friend advice you, make sure that you check it out with a professional consultation service before you decide on acting on it.

If you have to switch investment plans, do it with caution. Weigh the pros and cons before taking a decision.

The following points should help organize your thoughts:

- An analysis will help give you a comparison of your current investment plan and its alternatives. You should be able to get this done by a specially licensed financial advisor.
- Take stock of the current scheme you are on.
- Take into consideration your retirement plans. If you retire according to plan or earlier than planned, the scheme you opt for should be flexible enough to handle that.
- If you are in a public sector savings scheme, stay with it as it will not be affected by inflation and you stand to benefit in the long run.
- A personal savings scheme is vulnerable to fluctuations in the stock market and if you are not

into taking risks think carefully before opting for a change.

- There is a fee charged for switching schemes. If it is a small amount of money that needs to be changed to another scheme, this may not be practical as you may end up losing out.
- Keep in consideration the number of years left before retirement. Consider changing your savings scheme only if you have more than ten working years left.
- If you are considering changing to an overseas benefit scheme, it is prudent to check it out thoroughly. Make sure what you are getting into is not a scam. It is one of the important things to remember.

Having a good retirement plan in place will give you peace of mind. Choose the best scheme that gives you the best benefits so that you live out the rest of your years in comfort. Eliminate the worry of losing out because of fluctuating markets and inflation.

CHAPTER 3: FINANCIAL PLANNING BASICS

What does it mean to be financially fit?

To be financially fit doesn't mean merely having a regular job that pays well. It is not just about having several insurance policies to protect you against unexpected losses due to some fortuitous events. Neither is it limited to just having the means to cope with all of your family's financial obligations and needs. Being financially fit includes having plans in place for your financial needs in the coming years. It is also about having a plan for your children's future. But most especially, it is about building a nest egg you can bank on to be able to live comfortably once you retire from work.

Being financially fit is similar in many aspects to trying to be physically fit, where you have to be on the right track and do the right things to achieve your goals. It is not just about merely focusing on a desired outcome or zeroing in on a targeted goal. It is more about charting the correct path and staying on track all the while. It includes having well defined and achievable objectives to fuel your enthusiasm to remain on the path and not be sidetracked.

Financial fitness is not limited to achieving a targeted net worth nor accumulating a specific level of wealth. Rather, it is more about having a state of mind that is focused on setting the most appropriate financial goals, developing the most suitable financial plan, and incessantly working towards achieving them. However, you need to be financial literate to find the right path and start enjoying the benefits of being financially independent.

You have to realize that nothing is truly permanent in this world except change. There is no escaping it. It means even your current financial standing today is not likely to be the same financial position you will find yourself to be in tomorrow. It is going to turn out for the better or for the worse. There is no way you can stop change from taking place. The only thing you can do is to set the direction it should take and keep it that way.

The first step to achieving financial fitness is to undertake prudent financial planning. To do this, you need to have a strong determination, unwavering discipline, plus you have to be prepared to make a great deal of sacrifice. In exchange, the rewards you will reap will simply be remarkable.

Financial planning is all about the right approach and has little to do with financial expertise. Take a look at the step by step guide to master the basics in financial planning. This will not only help you manage your money better but lets you save a part of your earnings so that you can have a worry-free future.

Here are some easy to follow steps:

Step 1: Take an overall view of your finances

This doesn't merely mean stashing away your money in the bank or investing it either. It's about keeping a tab on every point through which your money leaves you as well as comes to you. Here are some of the points to be considered:

- Insurance premiums
- Active Loans
- Emergency funds
- Retirement savings
- Living Expenses

The above-mentioned aspects are the general costs borne by every earning individual, although it may not be limited to the same.

Constantly monitoring your finances shouldn't take up too much of your time, provided you do it on a regular basis. If you feel you require assistance, you can go ahead and get it, but make sure it is from a trusted source.

Step 2: Stick to a plan

Ensure you pay your insurance premiums, equated monthly installments regularly.

Make informed decisions when it comes to investing in stocks, shares, gold and so on. Never invest without knowing the risk you are getting signing up for.

Keep away some money for emergency reasons; you could either invest this sum in equity shares where you have the option of withdrawing on demand, or you could also keep a recurring deposit.

The money that is automatically deducted from your monthly salary is towards your provident fund which is meant to help you post retirement. It is vital that you never touch your PF money until you retire because this is a form of forced saving, and it should ideally start the moment you start earning.

By trying to focus on saving, don't be stringent on spending for essential things in life. The important thing is to categorize what's essential and what isn't.

Invest in equity only according to your needs and income; do not invest in high-risk shares expecting higher returns.

Step 3: Remember: Income - expenditure = savings

What this means is your expenses should not be more than your income for you to generate some savings.

Make sure you save at least 15% of your gross annual income, in your bank account. This should be a habit so that you have some money at your disposal as and when you want it.

The most ideal approach is to put part of your savings on autopilot using retirement plans such as your 401k. A clever way to do it is to increase your monthly contributions if you have not exhausted the maximum allowable monthly contributions for your 401K. Simply add an additional $50 to $100 each month to it. This will balloon over time, making a huge difference in your net worth at the time when you need it most.

Consider this. If your age now is 25 years old and you decided to add a hundred dollars each month to your 401k monthly contributions, you will have a whooping three hundred thirty thousand dollars ($330,000) extra money on your 401k account by the time you reach the golden age of 65. This is the conservative estimate on the returns of the add-on contribution based on 8% annual return which is a lot lower than the historical average long term returns of equities.

Don't forget though, that your add-on contributions are considered as pretax investments which means they will chip off $75 from your monthly paycheck for that $100 monthly add-on investment you put in (*that is, if you happen to be in the 25 percent bracket*).

The add-on money you put into your 401K account is automatically invested, that is why it is the easiest and most convenient way to save. The money gets invested without you laying your hands on it which means you will never have a chance to change your mind and spend it somewhere else.

Now, if you are lucky to have a very sympathetic and kind employer, he may just decide to put in a matching contribution, which means you'll end up with more free money in your savings to tidy you up during your golden years. But, if you happen to have already maxed your 401k, your best option is to make an automatic $333 monthly payment to an IRA account. Contact the nearest IRA office for assistance on how to set up automatic monthly payments.

Get to know more about how to raise your credit score so that you can avail the best-suited loans. For starters, search online to find out how to avail free debt consulting services and learn how to manage your finances better.

CHAPTER 4: HOW TO REDUCE YOUR INVESTMENT RISK THROUGH DIVERSIFICATION

Every investment portfolio is exposed to two types of risks, namely the Systematic Risk and the Individual Stock Risk.

The Systematic Risk is essentially an inherent market risk spawned by the market's volatility, and affects the whole financial market on the macro level or an entire segment of the market.

Since the measure of a stock's volatility in relation to the market is known as beta, this particular market risk has also become known as such. A good example of this macro level threat is recession where the ensuing economic downturn has a negative impact on the entire stock market.

This particular risk cannot be reduced, much less relieved through diversification. The only way to mitigate this risk is through a well calculated asset allocation strategy or through hedging.

The Individual Stock Risk is a stock-specific risk that refers to the possibility that a particular stock may perform below market expectations because of some internal issues such as the company goofing on an important business decision or a well-publicized business undertaking. The particular blunder may negatively impact the value of their stocks in the market, causing it to decline while the rest of the equities market continues to rise. This type of risk can be mitigated through diversification or by simply holding a diverse collection of different equities.

.on is choosing dissimilar investments in an
creasing returns and reducing overall portfolio
it is tempting to put all of your eggs into one
he hopes of striking it rich, this action can also
leau to ... ancial ruin as employees of Enron and WorldCom
experienced.

Since no amateur or professional can forecast the future of
the stock market, we are better off buying the entire market
through a low-cost index fund. This provides instant
exposure to every winner and every loser; thankfully, the
gains from the winners have outpaced the losses of the
failures.

The easiest way to achieve instant diversification from
company risk is through a mutual fund. The S&P 500 index
contains the stocks of 500 large-cap American companies.
By investing in a mutual fund, you eliminate the chance
that one company will wipe you out; however, is this
enough?

A mistake that many investors made in the latest financial
meltdown was assuming they were diversified because they
held several large-cap index funds. When the market
plunged, so did every fund they held. A more prudent
strategy is to include asset classes with low correlations to
one another.

Additional asset classes which investors may want to
consider include international funds, real estate investment
trusts, bond funds, and small cap funds. An investor who
put 100% of their assets into an S&P 500 fund in the year
2008 saw the value of their account plunge by nearly 50%.
However, an investor who invested 50% in an S&P 500
fund and 50% in a total bond market fund experienced a
roughly 25% drop in his or her portfolio. Also, they had the

opportunity to pick up shares dirt cheap by selling a portion of their bonds during the worst drop since the Great Depression.

Diversification allows investors to invest across a wide spectrum of asset classes which reduce overall risk and increase total return. The investor will experience fewer sleepless nights and less stomach acid compared to those less diversified.

Brokerage houses offer more selections at lower costs than ever before. It has never been easier to construct a well-diversified and low-cost portfolio than it is today. Consider adding index funds or ETF's focused on international markets, real estate investment trusts, or bonds. Through a well-diversified portfolio, you will increase the likelihood of reaching your financial goals while reducing the chance of financial ruin.

So far, we are aware of two different techniques to mitigate certain portfolio risks. We know that individual stock risks can be reduced through diversification. We also know that systematic risks can only be lowered through hedging. There is actually just a fine line that differentiates these two techniques and it is worth discussing further so we will have a better grasp of what diversification is really all about.

The idea behind diversification is to create an investment portfolio with multiple assets in order to lower the risk. Generally, the higher the number of assets that are in a portfolio, the lower the risk of the portfolio becomes. For example, if you have twenty different equities in your portfolio, and one or two of them are underperforming due to some management blunder, the rest of your holdings will remain unaffected. They will continue to generate earnings for you, mitigating the loss of the underperforming stocks in the process.

Now, if you park all your money in a single asset instead of distributing it among a basket of different assets, you are practically courting disaster. If, for some specific company blunder, the value of its stocks takes a nose dive, then your whole investment goes under with it.

Hedging, on the other hand, is about mitigating the systematic risk on an investment portfolio. It involves including two different assets that are negatively correlated to each other in the same portfolio to reduce the risk. It means whatever negative developments one of the assets goes through will be positive to the other.

A classic example of this is the negative correlation between the two different assets gold and equities. During times of severe political upheaval or economic crisis such as global recession, the price of equities takes a nose dive while the price of gold typically shoots up. This is the reason why gold is considered a safe haven for investible funds during times of crisis.

Diversification smoothens the overall performance of an investment portfolio by offsetting the negative results of a few underperforming assets with the positive gains resulting from the solid performance of the rest of the assets in the portfolio. There is a catch, though. You end up losing some of the potential gains made by your performing assets. This, however, is a fair enough trade-off since you will be reducing the overall risks your portfolio is exposed to.

Just imagine if you had placed all of your investments in a single asset that is severely underperforming. You are likely to lose most if not all of your investments. If you diversify, you may lose some of the potential gains but you will be giving your portfolio greater stability to weather volatile markets.

CHAPTER 5: ASSET ALLOCATION - WHEN INVESTING IS VERY IMPORTANT FOR YOUR FINANCIAL FREEDOM

Whether you believe it or not, asset allocation is vital for determining your financial freedom. Get it right and you will be rewarded handsomely with a profit producing portfolio. Get it wrong and you will be spinning your wheels while financial freedom will continue to elude you. All the different securities that a person could invest in are all collectively called assets or asset classes. As your savings increases, you will be purchasing more and more of these assets over time. So then the question becomes, exactly what asset classes are you going to purchase.

A very general rule of thumb here is to subtract your age from 100, and the answer represents what percent you will devote (allocate) to stocks (equities). The balance would then be allocated to bonds. So if you were just starting out in the investing world and you are 30 years old, you would allocate 70 percent of your portfolio to stocks and 30 percent to bonds. Simply put, this would be your asset allocation.

This 70-30 mix is not perfect though because usually you should leave a small portion of cash in your investing account to be able to take advantage of good opportunities that pop up from time to time in the marketplace. Maybe you want 5% in cash or 10% at most. Therefore, the final mix would look like this: 65% stocks, 30% bonds, 5% cash. Or 60% stocks, 30% bonds, 10% cash.

If, on the other hand, you are nearing your retirement years, say you are 55 years old, then your asset allocation should be 45% equities (100 – 55) and 55% on bonds. The idea is to put greater stability to your nest egg by cutting down your portfolio's exposure to the more volatile equities and shifting the weight in favor of the more stable bond issues. This is a form of asset allocation. You get the idea.

Asset allocation, like diversification, is an investment strategy that aims to balance the level of risk of a portfolio against the expected rewards. This is done by distributing available capital among different types of asset classes, while at the same time apportioning each asset according to targeted allocation percentages that suits the individual investor's risk tolerance, investment objectives, and the individual's set investment time frame.

From the previous chapter, we've learned that diversification is a strategy that aims to reduce the risk of an investment portfolio by distributing available capital among a larger number of different asset holdings. This time, we look at **asset allocation** as another strategy aiming to achieve the same goal of reducing investment risks.

Note that *asset allocation* employs a different approach. Instead of simply spreading the risk thinly among a large number of different assets, *asset allocation* reduces the risk thinly by distributing the investment among different classes of assets that are not closely related to each other.

An example of this type of distribution is a single portfolio that contains foreign stocks and domestic bonds - both of which belong to different categories of financial assets. The idea is to soften the impact of a possible price slide that may affect only one or two different classes of assets in particular. If one or two classes of assets decline, then the others will remain unaffected and will continue to make gains.

You may have heard that historically speaking stocks have a better rate of return than bonds. So then why not just put all your investment money into stocks? While that is a good deduction, the answer is also of a historical nature, and that is as follows: different asset classes perform differently in response to changing economic events and market factors.

A simple example of this can be seen when stocks are falling, bonds tend to rise as investors see them as a haven and flee from stocks and move into bonds. If you would like to achieve true financial freedom one day, then it would behoove you to invest across several different asset classes.

There are many other classes of investments that are not so correlated to equities which you may consider for inclusion in your asset allocation strategy. They include real estate, precious metals, rare and high valued collectibles, and financial derivatives, to name a few. Others even divide the equities market into different categories and consider each as a sub class where they apportion their investments in line with the concept of asset allocation - as long as they are not so correlated with each other.

For example, there are those who divide equities based on the size and market capitalization of the company issuing the shares of stocks; others prefer to segregate equities according to the industry sector or group to which the issuing company belongs such as technology, exchange traded funds, retail, mining, healthcare, food, utility, etc.; others divide equities according to their growth rate within the most immediate past, their current value in the spot market, and even the income earned in previous years;

others have a more general classification, separating local equities from those that are foreign issued.

In simple words, *asset allocation* refers to the investment strategy used by investors to apportion their investments among the different classes of financial assets. It is a crucial component of financial planning that aims to streamline investment portfolio in order to maximize returns for a particular level of risk.

The level of risk varies from one investor to another, depending on several factors like the individual's appetite for risk (risk tolerance), how long he intends to hold on to the portfolio (investment horizon), and his investment objectives and targeted goals.

As in our 70-30 principle, the younger the investor is, the bigger his risk tolerance is since he can hold on to his portfolio for a longer period of time. He is likely to have a more aggressive portfolio mix that is heavy on equities. Conversely, the more matured investors would be more interested in keeping their savings and their earnings intact as they approach their golden years. These investors are more likely to play it safe and veer more towards conservative portfolios that are heavy on bonds.

Asset allocation has a deeper and more profound effect on the returns that are expected to be generated by an investment portfolio - much more than the actual selection of assets to include in the portfolio, or the timing of the execution of trades. Studies have shown that 97% of the returns made by profitable portfolios can be credited to having the right asset allocation strategy.

Furthermore, purchasing different asset classes adds to the diversity of your portfolio and as everyone knows, you don't want to put all your eggs in one basket. More advanced investors would be spreading their assets over a larger mix of asset classes. For instance, one could purchase commodities, futures, options, etc. as a small percentage of your entire portfolio. Your Asset Allocation might look like this: 25% Domestic Equities (stocks), 25% Foreign Equities, 10% Corporate Bonds, 10% Government Bonds, 10% Municipal Bonds, 5% Commodities, 5% Precious Metals, and 10% Cash.

The last piece of the asset allocation puzzle involves a concept known as time horizon. When you are just starting out investing, you have a long time horizon. In other words, you won't need the money back real soon. As you get closer to your time horizon, you need to shift your asset allocation from an aggressive position to a position that does not have as much exposure to risk.

This is because of the possibility of a market downturn will leave you with not much time left to recoup your losses until you need the funds back for retirement. You accomplish this by shifting your asset allocation from one that is mostly stocked to one that is bonded. In our earlier example of 60-30-10 (stocks, bonds cash), you would reverse it over time so that by your retirement date, the portfolio would be 60% bonds, 30% stocks, and 10% cash. Your financial freedom will be dependent upon it so be sure to get this right!

CHAPTER 6: HOW TO DETERMINE YOUR ASSET ALLOCATION

The major factors that determine the returns on your investment are asset allocation, security selection, market timing and many other factors. In Asset allocation, you have to decide among various investment types i.e. stocks, bonds, cash equivalents, etc. It is indeed a big decision and around 90% of your portfolio performance depends on the asset allocation.

While determining the asset allocation, you should have proper knowledge on the various investment types. For example, you should know that stocks provide the highest returns among other assets; however, in this investment, you need to bear the greatest risk too. Bonds, on the other hand, provide significantly less risk, but in this type, the return is comparatively less too. Cash equivalents, which is a very short-term investment is almost risk-free.

Instead of picking only one of the three investment types, you should split your investment among the three asset classes to best utilize them. You should make the allocation depending on your expected return and also the amount of risk you are planning to bear. Economists have developed various models, which can tell you how different balances among the asset classes affect your risks and returns. To know more about the splitting, you should ask for some investment advice from the experts.

While making the best investment decisions and optimizing your asset allocation, you will have to consider some of your personal factors too. This includes:

a) Your age

b) Health condition

c) How much you need from your portfolio

d) Changes in life events.

These factors are important in the sense that, depending on these factors, you can determine the level of risk that you will be able to bear.

There are many formulas to determine the proper asset allocation. The most common formula among these is the Rule of Thumb. According to this formula, subtract your age from 100. Whatever value you get should be the percentage of your portfolio that should be invested in stocks. In the other sense, as you grow older, you should increase your investment in bonds.

There are some certain drawbacks of the rule of thumb since it doesn't consider your health and income level. Therefore, sometimes it may mislead you towards a wrong decision. However, this rule is far better than the investment advice from the brokers who advocate that major part of your investment should be in stocks and less than 10% in bonds.

To make the best investment decision, you will have to allocate your assets in any of the four portfolios mentioned below:

1. Low-risk level

2. Medium low-risk level

3. Medium-high-risk level

4. High-risk level

To determine the particular portfolio which will suit you the best, you need to study the historical records of each portfolio and make your judgment. However, the past result may not be reflected in the future environment. But, it will enable you to make some idea about the market movements.

CHAPTER 7: PASSIVE VS. ACTIVELY MANAGED INVESTING

Knowing the difference between active and passive investing will play a tremendous role in building wealth, as it will save you thousands of dollars over a long-term horizon. Active investing refers to a methodology whereby time is spent researching individual stocks that will make up your investment portfolio, over time these individual stocks will be churned in hopes of finding better investment opportunities.

One of the issues with active investing is the cost, transaction fees, or expense ratios if you are invested in a mutual fund. Also, diversification can be an issue as it will cost money and time to purchase the perfect stocks.

Passive investing, on the other hand, is a methodology that does not require constant churning, or tweaking as often as active investing. The best way to be a part of passive investing is by purchasing into index funds.

There are various funds which have been setup up to track the performance of the following indexes: S&P 500, Total Stock Market, Total Bond Market, Sectors, International Markets, etc. By investing in index funds that track the S&P 500, you essentially enjoy the performance of the publicly traded companies listed on the S&P 500. These funds are designed to offer diversification, as well as market returns.

At an average, the performance of the S&P 500 will outperform the performance of the majority of stock traders, and investment gurus. The issue is that many of these professionals have failed to outperform the market year over year. One year they may outperform the market and the next they underperform. By investing passively, and in index funds, you essentially set up yourself up to realize market returns, diversification, and free time that would otherwise have been spent researching and learning about individual stocks.

The best part of passive investing using index funds is their low expense ratio; many of the funds will have an expense ratio of 0.05% to 0.40%. While actively managed funds will have expense ratios of 0.5% to 1.5% although this may not seem like much of a difference, it can sure add up to a lot of money over a 10-year or a 20-year period.

Consider the fact that if you invest $10,000 into a fund that earns you a constant 8% return year over year for the next ten years, the difference between having your money into a fund with an expense ratio of 0.25%, and one that charges 1.0% is around $1,500. Your account would have $1,500 less at the end of the 10-year period if your money were invested in a fund with an expense ratio of 1.0%.

The $1,500 less is around 7% lower at the end of the period; this demonstrates the impact that fees can have on your investment portfolio. My calculation was done in a decade; it's much higher over a 20-year, or even a 30-year period. $1,500 may not seem like much when considering the time range. However, this fee could be higher if instead of investing $10,000, you invested $50,000, or even $500,000.

Bottom line, pay attention to your expense ratios as they can add up to a lot, and that any individual can start investing utilizing the passive methodology, and do well.

Passive investing is about beating 80% of investors while putting in only 3 to 5 hours of work a year.

It may sound improbable but it is definitely possible - you can beat 80% of investors while trading only 3 to 5 hours a year. The simple strategy you can use to achieve this is called passive investing. Some describe this investing strategy as a 'couch potato strategy' since it essentially involves buying and holding securities for the long term.

'Passive Investing' is in essence index investing where buying a share of the index fund allows you to own a broad spectrum of securities representative of various asset classes. It allows you to capture the returns of the whole market, which means it doesn't matter if one or several securities are lagging the market. What matters is making money over time from the collective return of all the assets that were pooled together into the index fund.

All you need to do after carefully selecting your basket of securities that will make up your passive investment portfolio is to just leave them there to appreciate in value through the years. But make no mistake about it because it is definitely not a 'set it and forget it' kind of thing. You need to review your portfolio regularly within a year to make sure the original weight you gave each asset class security remains the same. Changing market conditions may necessitate rebalancing your portfolio, which should take at least 3 to 5 hours each year.

So, how does this beat 80% of investors?

As discussed in an earlier chapter of this book, the vast majority of investors (80%) are actively managing their investments. They believe the market is inefficient and it does not immediately factor every market development into the price. That is why they are in constant search for undervalued securities so they can gain from possible short term price movements. In other words, they are timing the market hoping to generate better than market returns.

For varying reasons, these unfortunate investors have stubbornly stuck to their habit of constantly searching for undervalued securities and timing the markets. Sadly, history has always proven them wrong as evidenced by the fact that the returns they manage to get consistently lag the market year after year after year. Only about a little over 20% of them manage to beat the market occasionally.

It would then be easy to outperform the vast majority of these investors who actively manage their investments. How? By being a 'couch potato' investor - by taking the opposing view and going long term. This is exactly what passive investing is all about.

Passive investing (*in contrast to active investing*) is founded on the theory that the market is efficient. It factors all and every market development into the price without delay. This means there is no way a security will be undervalued or overvalued at any given time as current prices already reflect the security's fair value.

Over time, a security is bound to accumulate value. This puts to rest the argument of an inefficient market which all active investors adhere to – in short, there is no more need to actively buy and sell securities.

There are three main benefits of passive investing:

- It provides near-market returns.

- It makes portfolio diversification easy.

- It costs less than any active investing strategy.

As the securities market gets more and more efficient information with the advent of new technologies, active investors will find it more difficult to make money. Passive investing, on the other hand, can be expected to continue outperforming active investing over time. Meanwhile, stock picking will slowly become a thing of the past.

CHAPTER 8: MUTUAL FUND INVESTING - INDEX VERSUS MANAGED - WHICH IS BEST?

Mutual funds investors are always confronted with the decision about investing in managed funds or using an index fund. There are plenty of people who believe one is better than the other, so we will review the advantages and disadvantages of each and I will provide my suggestion to help you out.

Actively Managed Funds: All mutual funds that are actively managed by a fund company to add value to shareholders returns fall into this category. In theory, an experienced portfolio manager can surpass the returns of an index fund by making well-timed and disciplined trades. Unfortunate, the vast majority of fund managers do NOT beat their index. But the good news is that the top 20% of these funds can and do on a regular basis. We will try to focus on this group of quality managers.

Advantages: The main advantage of active management is that quality managers use their experience, analytical skills, and economic research to help find undervalued investments that are ready to outperform the market. They can focus their buying on the areas that they find most attractive and sell or avoid those that are under-performing. An active manager can take advantage of market dips to buy or sell as necessary which can add value to your investment.

A great management team can add several percentage points to your overall return each year, and this can add up over time. Your net returns, even after higher expense charges, can be noticeably higher than an index fund.

Disadvantages: Along with the increased buying and selling activities of an active manager comes a higher expense charge for those trading and management costs. Most actively managed funds have a 50 to 100% higher operating expense ratio than the average index fund. If you are not getting better returns, this can cost plenty over time. Also, if your quality manager leaves the fund, you may need to find a better alternative.

Index Funds: Any fund that is made up of a static portfolio structured to mirror the investments of a proposed market index is classified as an index fund. There are small cap indices, bond indices, international indices, specialty indices and many others. The most widely used are the S&P 500 index where the fund uses the same 500 stocks that are included in the Standard and Poor's 500. These portfolios are only changed when and if the index changes its holdings which allow for a very tax efficient, low turnover investment.

Advantages: Index funds provide a static and very transparent investment portfolio. They also offer very low turnover of securities due to less buying and selling. This allows them to keep operating expenses at a minimum and usually substantially lower than their managed counterparts. The fact that they represent the entire stock or bond holdings of the index provides great diversification, which can also be a disadvantage.

Disadvantages: Because these funds are not actively managed, you cannot weed out under-performing securities from the overall index. This can and does have a detrimental effect on your returns. If market conditions warrant action, index funds usually will not be altered unless it happens to coincide with their regular rebalancing schedule.

If you are thinking that because you own several of the most popular index mutual funds, your investment portfolio is already properly diversified; you may be in for some rude re-awakening. Having several funds in your portfolio mix is not a guarantee that you have covered all the bases. If fact, it may result in fund overlaps which can effectively reduce the benefits of diversification.

Fund overlaps result from having two or more funds that have positions in the same securities. This can kneecap your entire investment portfolio, especially if those same securities present in two or more of your funds suffer a negative loss. In other words, it unnecessarily exposes you to greater risks since you are holding on to more of the same kind of security.

It negates the primary reason why you need to diversify – which is to have adequate downside protection. It protects your portfolio from going under in case one sector goes haywire and delivers poor performance. Having fund overlaps also mean part of your capital is unnecessarily tied to the same security, effectively limiting your upward exposure.

Having fund overlaps is unavoidable, particularly if you obtain different funds from different companies with different managers. Each one of these fund managers is likely to include the most popular and most profitable security in their respective mixes, causing a fund overlap if you include them in your portfolio mix. Small amounts of overlaps are tolerable. However, extreme overlaps can turn your portfolio into a lame duck.

What you need to do

There is no easy way to check for overlaps. The best thing to do is to check each fund every quarter and compare the top holdings of each fund with one another. If two or more of the funds have overweighed the same security, then you may consider retaining only one of the funds and replacing the other (or others) with another fund (or funds).

Checking for overlaps in your mutual fund holdings can be difficult and tedious. You can pay for a service to check for overlaps or you can manually analyze and compare the top holdings of each of your funds.

It is easier, though to avoid overlaps if you are just starting your investment portfolio. The secret is to choose funds with different objectives. That way, you can be almost sure that there won't be an overlap in their top holdings.

CHAPTER 9: THE INFAMOUS RULE OF 72 ON INVESTING

(Or How to Double Your Money in 7 to 10 Years)

Every investment guru will tell you that if you simply park your money and leave it untouched in a portfolio containing a mix of any non-speculative, dividend earning, and stable investments, it will eventually double its value after a specific period of time. This is not magic or an empty promise. This is a mathematical probability that uses the power of *compounding interests.*

Ask any investment banker or financial adviser you know and they will tell you it is true. They have had this knowledge for a long time, yet for some reason they seem to be hiding it from us. This infamous mathematical probability is called the Rule of 72.

The Rule of 72 is basically a mathematical shortcut meant to determine the future value of a certain amount. Specifically, it calculates the length of time it will take an investment to double in value if it is left to grow with compounding interest. According to the rule, if you divide the number 72 by the annual rate of return, it will give you the length of time for your money to double with the given rate.

Mathematically, the Rule of 72 is expressed as follows:

Annual Rate multiplied by Number of Years (for it to double) = 72

If the annual rate is given, you can get the Number of Years (for it to double) with this:

Number of Years (for it to double) = *72 divided by the given Annual Rate*

If you want to know at the rate you will double your money for a given number of years you can use this:

Annual Rate = 72 divided by desired Number of Years

Following the formula above, you will arrive at 7.2 years for your money to double its value at 10% compounded annual rate of return (72/10%). Similarly, you can calculate that it will take 10 years for your money to double at 7.2% (72/7.2).

Clearly, the ball is really on your side of the court. As indicated by the calculations above, it is highly possible for you to double your money within 7 to 10 years - but for that to happen, you need to invest your money in a portfolio mix that gives an annual collective yield of between 7.2% and 10% c.

Using this as your basis therefore, what you need to do is to carefully put together a mix of investment instruments which have demonstrated their consistency in providing similar yields in the past. The bottom line is - it still is your call.

Your choices of where to put your money will actually depend a lot on what kind of an investor you are - as well as on your appetite for taking risks.

If you are the conservative kind with no appetite for risk taking, then your portfolio must only include investments that are considered relatively safe and stable. This can be a diversified mixture of blue chip stocks and investment grade bonds.

Blue chip stocks are those issued by financially stable and well-established companies with billions of dollars in capitalization. These companies are not likely to go under in the near term. They are also known for paying increasing dividends through the years (some even for decades).

On the other hand, investment grade bonds are municipal or corporate bonds with high (*AAA to AA*) to medium (*A to BBB*) credit rating and are therefore thought to be least likely to default.

Let's assume that you have a portfolio mix made up evenly of blue chips stocks and investment grade bonds. If the blue-chip stocks in your portfolio have an average annual yield of 10% and your investment grade bonds have an annual return of roughly 6%, then these two should collectively give you a net return of 8%. Using the Rule of 72 formula, you divide 72 by the net return (8%) to get 9 years - the length of time to keep your money invested in this mix for it to double its value - and 18 years to quadruple it.

The speculative investors may, however, find the waiting time of 7 to 10 years too long and too boring. They are the types of investors who are willing to face bigger risks for bigger pay-offs. They are fully aware of the fact that in investing, the bigger the risks you take, the bigger the rewards will be.

Because they are in a hurry to supersize the value of their investments, they prefer to put their money on the more volatile stock options, delve on highly leveraged trading, or get engrossed with picking penny stocks. These are the types of investment where you can double your money overnight or lose your shirt just as fast.

Some words of caution though. If it's a nest egg you want to build for the future which you are looking forward to helping you go through your golden years comfortably, then it's best to avoid being speculative. Set your sights instead on placements that will provide you with reasonable and stable annual returns with less risk.

And in case somebody comes along trying to convince you to join their speculative bandwagon by showing you his almost spotless trading records, put one thing in your mind – "A sterling performance in the past is not a guarantee of future results." Resist the temptation to turbo-charge your investments and stay conservative. Your money is bound to eventually double in time anyway so why take the extra risks?

Below is a Rule of 72 chart showing the type of returns that will double your money over a corresponding period of time. This may help you in your search for the best placements for your money that will double it in time.

% Annual Investment Yield		Number of Years to Double your Money		72
3	X	24	=	72
4	X	18	=	72
5	X	14.4	=	72
6	X	12	=	72
7	X	10.2	=	72

8	x	9	=	72
9	x	8	=	72
10	x	7.2	=	72
11	x	6.5	=	72
12	x	6	=	72
13	x	5.5	=	72
14	x	5.1	=	72

CHAPTER 10: THE KEY STEPS TO SUCCESS IN REAL ESTATE INVESTMENT

If one wants to successfully invest in the property market be it residential or commercial during an economic down turn, then this can be a difficult task. With property prices spiraling downwards and the few buyers that are out there in the market that does have the financial support or capital to buy simply will not pay competitive prices for property.

Due to this situation, it is essential if you are considering investing in property, to fully understand current market conditions to achieve the greatest returns on your property investment. Property investment has long been a popular type of investment which, in theory, simply involves a process of buying property to rent later out to tenants or customers and in the end sell on at for a profit.

Unfortunately, in an unstable economy as we find ourselves in currently, achieving this success with this type of investment can prove to more elusive and more difficult, then the simple purchasing and leasing / renting of properties. All new investors must fully understand that to achieve their success with this type of investment; success is dependent on their ability to wisely and carefully make their investment in real estate.

Investment in property involves the investing one's money into the property with the aim of making a profit. In generally, these investments are concerned with the buying of properties, renting to consumers or tenants and at some future date selling them when prices are high to make a profit on the appreciated market value. Real estate can mean any brick and mortar building or property located on land which is bought and sold. It can range from an apartment/office building to smaller structures like storage units or garages.

To achieve success in real estate investment, there are several steps to follow. Let us go through the important key steps to follow:

1. You must choose your Market

As an investor, you will want to choose a market in which you hope to be the most successful. It will not matter if you are buying, selling, or renting, as business is more likely to be profitable for you when you are working in a market that best suits your personal needs.

2. Determining your Plan

It is essential for you to decide what it is that you hope to achieve with your investment in real estate. Without determining this it will be hard for you to progress with your plans. For some investors, they will decide to rent their investments out for long periods while for others they will prefer to renovate them and then sell them on when the market is high.

It does not matter which avenue you choose, as there is always room to profit in all markets. However, your plan must be in place before starting out, as it lets you make decisions about your property investment when the profitable opportunities appear.

3. Talk to the Professionals

Remember that when you are stating on in real estate investing, there is a lot to learn. A good place to start and get the best advice is a professional real estate investment course. These assist you in achieving the success you strive for with your entry into the property investment market. By studying and learning all the specialized techniques of the business, you are better prepared for what lies ahead.

These professional traders can combine their knowledge and practical experience and will share this with you so that you can integrate what you learn into your personal strategies.

4. Execution

When you have studied all that you can and feel ready to commence with your real estate investment plan, then you must execute the plan. You have already prepared yourself for success, so all that is needed is to execute your investment plan in line with the decision you have made and the and information you have learned.

5. Education

One should note that these investment courses are not only a source of professional strategies, but they also arm you with essential and beneficial information about the ins and outs of the real estate investment industry. For, if you truly plan on achieving success with your investments, you should be fully prepared like a soldier to war when setting out on your journey to success. Attending professional real estate investment courses achieve this for you and it is well worth considering in order to leverage your possibilities of success.

If you ask the most experienced investors where to park your money to realize better long term gains, their common answer will be real estate. Having sad that, let us explore the many ways we can invest on real estate.

1. You can put your money on publicly listed real estate investment trusts (REITs). REITs are investment vehicles that function much like a mutual fund. Its financial resources pooled from several investors are used to invest on commercial, industrial, or residential buildings, specifically buying, selling, developing, leasing or renting them out.
    The REITs' main source of revenue comes from the property leases, from the rent, and other fees collected from their various property holdings. They also earn interest from mortgage properties they own. Another source of revenue is the appreciation in real property value of the underlying assets they manage.

    There are two ways you can invest on REITs. You can buy REIT shares directly in the spot market or you can invest your money on mutual funds whose focus is on public real estate.

    Surprisingly, America's young adults have shown an uncanny interest on real estate investing. These millennials know fully well that real investing can provide them with an additional source of monthly income aside from providing a hedge against inflation. But instead of buying actual real estate properties, they instead put their money on real estate investment trusts (REITs).

    The reason why millennials are more interested on REITs is because it allows them to invest on real estate properties without the worries of real home ownership commitments tying them down. They enjoy the flexibility of being able to move around from one work place to another looking for greener pastures where they can establish their roots. At the same time, they are able to generate extra income monthly to help them pay off their student loan obligations.

2. If there are publicly listed REITs, there are also private REITs. Private REITs are also known as private placements. They provide much higher returns than the public REITs, but only a chosen group of investors are given the opportunity to invest in them. Some of the private REITs that give the best returns are exclusively offered to investors who meet the strict accreditation standards they set.

   For example, to qualify for the private REITs giving the best returns, the investor must have a net worth of one million dollars or those primary home owners whose annual income for the past two years is $200,000.

   The qualifying standards are so strict that only a few investors are able to get accreditation. Most of them invest with these private placements but also enjoy the benefit of investing on a financial instrument with sufficient safeguards that lower investing risks.

3. There are investors who have the means to purchase real estate properties outright and who prefer to own the actual asset than put their money on trusts. These investors 'flip real estate properties'. They pour in their capital to purchase cheap real estate properties such as those on the auction block, then make the necessary improvements to up their values.

They then sell the properties or rent them out at a much higher price. The main consideration of the investors who 'flip houses' and other real estate properties is the projected cash flow the property can generate.

4. For some, a simple way of investing on real estate is to buy the property they choose to live in rather than continue renting one. This way, they are able to build their equity on the property through the monthly payments they make. They can then sell the property at a profit later on.

CHAPTER 11: PRECIOUS METALS WE SHOULD INVEST IN

Precious metals are known to be rare metallic chemical elements and, throughout history, they have been used for different purposes. These elements are considered to be of high economic value and nowadays the most common metals in the monetary market are gold and silver. But when we refer to precious metals, then ruthenium, rhodium, palladium, osmium, iridium and platinum must also be recalled in this area.

Gold is the most popular metal which is used in the jewelry industry, but it is also known for its important role in medicine, electronics, dentistry, and food industry. In the present, this metal is seen more as a real investment, because the current money system is going through a period of stress and more and more people believe that investing in precious metals will be a safe method for the future.

If you decided to invest in gold, you should adopt the best strategy and try to find the most profitable way, based on your needs. You can resort to the physical gold method of investment, which includes coins, bars, and jewelry, or choose the gold exchange-traded funds and the gold stocks.

Silver also has a special place in both coinage and jewelry systems, and it is well appreciated for its high electrical conductivity. This metal has an important role in the manufacturing of musical instruments and dental fillings, or in the mechanical ventilation. Like gold, silver was used as a currency, but compared with gold, the price of silver is rather uncertain.

There are numerous ways in which you may invest in silver, and if you do not know what choice to make, then you should ask for an expert's opinion. If you prefer a traditional method of investment, you could choose silver bullion bars, but if you would like to search for a new form of trading, then invest in silver coins. Other methods could be those of exchange-traded funds, bank accounts, shares in mining companies and more.

Due to the present effects of the financial crisis, investing in precious metals could be the best choice. When most people think of investing in precious metals, they usually choose the bullion method of investment, but this strategy varies depending on each requirement.

Even if platinum and palladium are also used for different purposes, gold and silver remain the reliable factors of investment itself. For those who are already used to invest in these metals, they are a means to increase their portfolio and a trusted source for the future.

However, even if the demand for precious metals keeps on rising, it doesn't necessarily mean there will be an immediate spike in price. It depends a lot on their constantly changing supply levels, resulting from active mining as well as the aggressive selling by large stake holders.

You have to do quite a bit of your own research before making your purchases. You also have to provide a storage space that is safe and secure if you elect to park your money on coins or bullion. Investing on precious metals requires maintaining a long-term perspective, meaning you have to be prepared to weather short term market volatility.

Investing in Gold

There are many ways to invest in gold. You can <u>invest in</u> <u>physical gold</u> by buying gold coins, jewelry or other physical forms of the metal. You may invest in gold by buying shares of stock in gold mining companies. There are also Exchange Traded Funds that track spot gold prices (Gold ETFs) which you can include in your investment portfolio.

The most popular and the most convenient way of investing in gold is by buying or selling gold futures through commodity exchanges such as the New York Mercantile Exchange or COMEX. You can either trade directly with the exchange via their regular brokers, or trade online via their online brokers using a virtual trading platform.

For retail investors, it would be wise to do online trading instead of opening a direct trading account with the exchange. It requires less capital and the trading hours are longer.

To start trading gold futures, all you need to do is open an online account with a member broker of the exchange. In the case of gold, your options can be any online broker accredited by CME Globex, India's NCDEX, Dubai's DGCX, Multi Commodity Exchange, or Tokyo Commodity Exchange.

Once an account holder, you will be provided with a virtual trading platform which is linked to the global gold market in real time. Using this platform, you'd be able to buy gold futures or trade on spot prices of gold in real time with minimal margin requirements.

Most online brokers use the Metatrader 4 as their virtual trading platform. This is one of the most popular, user-friendly trading platforms around. It allows you to trade any of the many securities serviced by your broker-provider, using only just one account. This trading platform comes with a powerful array of technical analysis tools and real time financial news feed to help you make trading decisions with less difficulty.

Gold futures (*including current month or spot gold*) are traded by lots. Each lot is equivalent to 100 ounces of gold. Some brokers offer micro and e-mini accounts where lot sizes are smaller (10 ounces and 1 ounce lots) compared to regular accounts where 1 lot is equivalent to 100 ounces of gold.

Nymex gold has a ticker symbol of GC while its electronic trading counterpart under CME Globex is EGC. CME Globex E-Micro Gold future has a ticker symbol of MGC.

Trading is highly leveraged with margins as low as 1% of the notional value of the contracts. Maximum leverage for gold micro account can be as high as 1:1000. However, current regulations in the U.S. limited the leverage for margin trading to no more than 1:50.

Minimum contract size for micro accounts is 10 ounces with minimum $0.10 per ounce price increments. Margin call is set at 40% of the notional value. Automatic cut point is at 10%NV. (*Notional value = number of ounces x current price / 100*). For regular accounts, initial margin requirements start at $2000 for every position taken.

Current Gold Outlook

Gold prices have been plummeting for the last 2 ½ years, losing 27% of its value and dropping by more than 38% from its September, 2011 high of $1,923.70 per ounce. The main contributing factor to this horrendous drop in prices is the improving U.S. and global economies which triggered the capital flight from safe haven to more meaningful investments – a logical move expected to happen when the economic outlook is all pink and roses. However, the question is after 2 ½ years of stormy down trend, has it reached bottom and ready to mount another rally?

By all indications, gold has lost its luster as a safe haven for investment funds, and investors are not likely to get on board any time soon. All things considered, what will come into play is the demand-supply equation. With gold production dwindling consistently and as the demand for gold remains constant, it won't be long before the short supply of gold gets back its firm hold of the market.

The fact remains that the total gold supply dropped by 3% last year and the supply crunch is predicted to continue for another year or so, which may trigger another gold uptrend in the near term. However, bottom picking is tricky and should be done with extreme care and only after an exhaustive analysis of current price movements.

Silver Facts

Silver is like gold in many respects, particularly as an investment vehicle. The price movement of silver is more volatile, though since market liquidity is 18 times lower than gold. This means even single volume transactions can have a profound impact on silver prices. Worst, large traders or investors have the potential of influencing the movement of silver prices. Under normal market conditions, silver tracks gold prices with a ratio of 1:50 gold/silver.

The physical demand for silver is estimated at a mere $15.2 billion per year. However, the industrial uses of silver are on the rise from the silver-based biocides found in almost all industrial, consumer, and commercial products to the latest technology using Nano-silver particles with applications that include bone cement, wound dressings, surgical masks, surgical instruments, and lately as silver particles on the surface of home appliances.

The regular silver futures have the ticker symbol of SI with a contract size of 5,000 ounces per lot and requires an initial margin deposit of $11,000 with a maintenance margin requirement of $10,000.

The micro silver future, on the other hand, has a ticker symbol of SIL and has a contract size of only 1,000 ounces per lot. The initial margin requirement is $2,200 per lot with a maintenance margin requirement of $2,000.

Silver Outlook

Analysts believe there will be little investment appetite for silver especially after shedding 35% of its value from mid-December, 2013 prices despite the growing demand for it from the industrial sector. It will continue to track the price of Gold which is currently also in the doldrums.

CHAPTER 12: COMMON INVESTING MISTAKES BEGINNERS MAKE

Whether investing money to the tune of $1000, $10,000 or much more, there are basic investing mistakes that most beginners make. These mistakes can be very costly, so let's look at investing $10,000 and how beginners can do things right.

When investing money, beginners must realize that there is no such thing as a perfect investment. You can't have it all in any one single investment. If you are investing $10,000, you must have your personal financial objectives in mind. What are your priorities from this list: high liquidity, safety, growth, higher income, tax advantages?

Be honest with yourself and your financial planner if you have one. Investing money is all about tradeoffs, and what level of risk you are willing to accept.

Of all the investing mistakes beginners make, not knowing and sticking with your financial objectives is the worst. If you are investing $10,000, do you need instant access to your money (high liquidity) in case you have a financial emergency? If so you need a safe investment like a money market fund; and you give up growth, higher income and tax advantages.

Otherwise, you could be faced with fees and penalties, or market losses if you need to cash in at the wrong time. For example, you don't want to be forced to liquidate a $10,000 stock investment that's fallen to $5000 just to make your mortgage payments.

Once you have your objectives in mind, get a handle on the investment options that fit your needs before you start investing money. For example, if you are working for a living and investing for retirement, you need at tax break and should consider an IRA or your 401k plan at work if you have access to one.

If you are investing $10,000 a year you might want to put half in such a plan and the other half someplace you can get to it without penalties. Lack of liquidity is one of the most common investing mistakes beginners make.

Avoid excessive costs and fees. Investing money in stock funds and bond funds to get growth and income does not need cost you an arm and a leg. Investing $10,000 in the wrong mutual funds could cost you $500 off the top when you invest and as much as $200 or more EACH YEAR for expenses and other fees. This is one of those investing mistakes beginners make that can be costly over time.

For example, people invest in bonds to earn a higher income, and over the long-term, bonds have returned about 6% a year. You can't afford to give a third or half of that back in charges and fees. Go with no-load index funds. There are no sales charges to invest, and investing $10,000 can cost less than $50 a year, period.

Investing money successfully need not be a part-time job, but it does require a little ongoing effort on the investor's part. Ignoring the status of their investments is a common investing mistake beginners and many other investors make. Look at your quarterly statements when you get them. Are there charges and fees you don't understand, are you losing money? You cannot correct a problem if you don't know it exists.

It's no big secret that most investors achieve stunningly poor returns on their money. Some of them even end up with drastically impaired capital, while a significant number lose theirs completely. Obviously, there is something they are not doing right. One of the most foreboding thing about investing is every mistake you make can drastically impact investment returns and may even lead to a significant loss of your capital.

Therefore, it will definitely help you a great deal to know exactly what these investors are doing wrong so you can avoid falling in the same dire investing predicaments.

Getting started, here are some of the many mistakes most investors commit:

Investing without an investment strategy or plan

Any form of investment can be likened to journeying through rough seas. An investment strategy is what serves as your navigational map which will guide you in reaching your destination. Without such a map, it may be impossible to cross the 'rough seas' (the market) and reach your destination (your investment objectives). You may end up somewhere else you don't want to be.

Investing for a living or with a "Paycheck Mentality"

It will be disastrous to start investing hoping you'll earn enough to replace your paycheck. Many have tried doing it by becoming day traders. It forces you to engage in short term plays - buying and selling stocks feverishly in an attempt to make small gains from short term price movements.

Unfortunately, getting in and out of the market more frequently comes at a stiff price – the outlandish fees you have to pay your brokers and the higher risk exposure. Besides, it is very rare for short term players to outperform the market. And if ever they do, they still end up underperforming once you deduct the aggregate brokers' fees that pile up.

What you need is a long-term plan, particularly if your portfolio is meant to tidy you up during your golden years. As one successful investor once said "you must treat your investment decisions as if you only have 15 trades to make throughout the life span of each investment".

Putting all your eggs in one basket by failing to diversify

Many investors tend to put all their money on stocks of companies belonging to the same industry. Such a move is quite risky because if anything adverse happens, the whole portfolio will go down with it.

The best thing to do is to thin out your risk exposure by broadly diversifying your holdings – spreading your money on different asset classes and not just on one. It is also important to strike a balance in your holdings such that you achieve maximum gains with the less risks.

Investing in stocks without doing due diligence on the company

Many investors invest in stocks because they simply like it or in a spur of the moment thought perhaps influenced by the stock's most recent favorable price movements, without doing some due diligence work or without assessing the company's financial standing and its profit potential in the long term.

Making a stock or a bond pick out of whims or without careful evaluation is a perfect formula for disaster.

You pay too much attention on media broadcasted financial advice

Stock or bond picks taken from financial news shows will not really help you achieve your goals. They are mostly done with hindsight. If you reflect on the wisdom of it, do you think anyone who has a profitable investment tip or a secret formula will announce it on live television?

For sure, they would rather keep it to themselves and make their millions than continue making a living blabbering in the boob tube or publishing financial newsletters with investing tips.

Buying high, selling low

People often try to jump in or out of a bandwagon too late. They observe the rise of rallying stocks with guarded caution and only make their decision to buy after it's ready to peak. Or, they hold on to 'losers' too long in the hope that they will bounce back so they can at least break even only to dispose them at a bigger loss after realizing too late that the slide is bound to continue.

As a result, they either buy high or sell low, which is contrary to the main trading dictum which is to buy low and sell high.

Predicting short term market movements

Almost all investors try to time their entry into or exit from a trade by predicting short term market movements. They are more often than not - always wrong. The best way is to evaluate the long term potential of a security to make profits then buy and hold.

Going the way of the high-frequency traders

High frequency traders buy and sell securities more often than they change their underwear. No less than investing icon Warren Buffet warned us against this when he said you are making a big mistake if you are trading actively. He is a firm believer in buying and holding a security for the long haul.

You can avoid the common investing mistakes beginners make and put yourself in a better financial position. Know your financial objectives and get a handle on your investment options. Keep your cost of investing low and stay on top of your investments. Once you have cash reserves set aside for liquidity, you can start spending money one step ahead of the crowd.

PUTTING IT ALL TOGETHER

There is a lot of information about investment trading. If this is one area that you would like to explore for yourself, one of the very first points you should settle from the start is what you will be trading. Tackling this is the only way you can take the right steps to isolate the best resources to help you get started.

Several markets are great for investors. Among your best market options are stocks, options, CFDs, commodities, and currencies. If you take a look around at where the top investors are, you might see that many of them have investments in two or three markets. You shouldn't follow the same step as a beginner.

You might think that the best investments are those that are diversified. Most likely, you're thinking that the more diverse your portfolio, the lower your risks of losing. This might initially seem logical since different markets have different risk levels. One loophole to this reasoning, however, is that you will understandably be unable to gain mastery over any market.

Let's clarify things. Investing can get pretty complicated regardless of the market you're in. You need to learn loads of technical terms and processes. Moreover, you also need to build up your instinct for detecting good trades. What this implies is that you need a large amount of time and effort to learn the ins and outs of just one market. Once you dive into wide investment trading, you could lose all you have because you don't have the level of skill and knowledge needed to get you through.

What you should want to know is which market is the ideal one to get into first. Logically, you should start learning the ropes in a market that you are at ease with. You'll find out which market this is if you start reading about each to get a feel for what is easiest for you to learn and understand.

Many specialists would point out that the easy path is to trade stocks first. Obviously, this doesn't mean that stock trading is simple. Among all the markets, though, the stock market is the most clear-cut. Also, you will find that there are quite many excellent resources for you to access and use. There are more than a handful of expert references and tools that you can tap for stock trading to help you make the best investments possible.

There is also a lower degree of risk in the stock market than in any other market. Take note that no one is spared from the possibility of losing a lot in this market. Stock traders, however, do lose less than those in other markets who invest just about the same amount of cash. This is because stocks, unlike currencies, are not leveraged. Keep in mind that high leverage assets can yield huge profits for small investments but also present the risk of huge and quick losses.

The actual secret to earthly wealth is in investment trading. You can only ensure great profits though if you make sure you make the right market choice. Don't trade everything. Settle on only one market and master it.

Thanks for downloading this book. It is my firm belief that it has provided you with all the answers to your **Investing** questions.

I hope you have benefited from this book. I would greatly appreciate if you could leave a review on Amazon.

Made in the USA
San Bernardino, CA
20 January 2017